The Forgotten Light

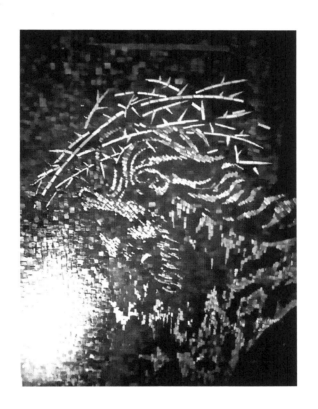

Annie Q. Porco

Table of Contents

I dedicate this book to
Joseph Paul Boyachek
Lead Pastor at Richview Church

His message to us all,

Keep fighting with chutzpah
to bring Love and Light to this broken world.

June 27, 1976 - November 26, 2018

The Forgotten Light

Looking down at the work he created with his own hands, he would ask himself the following questions; why was such a man of pure love forgotten? Why do some believe this man did not even exist? Have we lost our light of hope?

The dark image he created on the mosaic was not easily recognized, but it had tremendous power and a life of its own; this image now had a purpose and a mission.

Zbyszek created the mosaic in his early years during the hippie era. Zbyszek, who was nicknamed, Ziggy was born in Poland. As a young adult he was very involved with the arts and music.

Ziggy was a free spirit and enjoyed hitchhiking with his friends very much. Numerous times he would go hitchhiking on his own just so that he could spend time reflecting and connect with himself on a deeper level.

During those lonely excursions, Ziggy would often think about what was happening to the world and where was humanity heading. Being a man of faith he could not comprehend why people were still acting in such a destructive way.

During his time as a hippie, Ziggy became discouraged and depressed about life. When he was in a depressed state his artistic creativity was at its best!   It was during this time that he decided to create a mosaic of Jesus Christ.

With feelings of disappointment and hopelessness lingering, Ziggy decided to make an incredible mosaic of Jesus Christ. During that time, he was deeply affected and sad as to what was occurring around the world.

Ziggy would ask himself why humanity had become so destructive, selfish, violent, and warlike. He felt that many were influenced by the outside world. People seemed to be more concerned with what they could achieve and what they could loose, instead of what good they could do for humanity and for the world. He felt that If we could all let love lead the way, what a wonderful world it would be!

Ziggy was a big part of the hippie movement. He was a cross between a hippie, and a Bohemian. He also was a free spirit. Bohemians were more in line with Ziggy's beliefs, which followed Christ's teachings of peace and love towards your fellow being. Like most hippies, Ziggy also had long hair and a beard.

It was during this time that Ziggy was inspired to make a mosaic of Jesus Christ. It was coincidental that Jesus and hippies looked alike, having long hair and beards. He felt that Bohemians and hippies (especially Bohemians) not only had similar philosophies with the teachings of Christ, but as well a similar image.

During that era Ziggy started to feel disheartened. He kept pondering what the future held. The world was so divided; could people ever live together in peace and harmony? Feeling tremendous sorrow Ziggy came to realize that there were no solutions for what was going on in the world. The only way for him to live his life was to just, let it be.

At times, Ziggy would hear soft loving words coming from his heart and soul, saying, "love is in each and every one of us, we must let love lead the way, and in time there will be an answer".

Listening to these silent words in his mind Ziggy felt torn. He was feeling so much hope for humanity, but at the same time he felt such sadness because there was so much hatred in the world. Jesus teachings after all were all about loving one another.

Ziggy at this time was in turmoil. His feelings
would change often from feelings of hope and then
feelings of despair. In his saddest moments he
would think of Jesus and his powerful words. He
knew that Jesus was all about love, peace, and
kindness.

Ziggy would continually ask himself why people were not hearing and following the teachings of Christ. What was happening around the world no longer made any sense to him. The only thing that did make any sense to him was the power of love.

The teaching of Jesus was the only truth for Ziggy. He wanted to live his life following Jesus's footsteps. He had tremendous devotion towards Christ, and that is what drove him to create a mosaic in His image. He wanted to make something extraordinary that he could always have, and that would always keep the light of hope in his heart.

When Ziggy decided to make the mosaic he felt demoralized about life. His deepest feelings were coming from a place of love for humanity and the loss of hope for them. In this state of confusion and uncertainty he began to make the mosaic.

Ziggy designed the picture of Jesus with a crown of thorns on His head which represented pain and suffering. To make the mosaic he used very small pieces of brown wood which accidentally created a feeling of dark misery to the image.

The tiny pieces of wood Ziggy used were all of the similar colour and had no shine to them at all, which made the image of Jesus difficult to recognize. However, that is what made the mosaic so incredible, one had to really focus in order to see Christ in the mosaic.

At first when Ziggy started making the mosaic his feelings for humanity were of sadness, and hope, but as he continued working on the mosaic his feelings started to slowly shift. He started to feel a great love for mankind. This in turn gave him a true sense of peace.

After the masterpiece was finished Ziggy decided to show it to his family, and they were all amazed at how beautiful it looked. Ziggy was grateful with the way it turned out, but, he did notice that the mosaic was very dark in colour, and it was in great need of light.

What was mournfully interesting about the mosaic was that, you were looking at the pain and suffering that Jesus endured.

The mosaic was very precious to Ziggy. Over the years many people offered to buy it, but he knew that he could not put a price on it. This mosaic was now a part of him, and it was to remain at his side always.

When Ziggy got married he brought the mosaic to his new home and hung it where everyone could enjoy it. However, every time he looked at it he felt a bit disappointed as he still thought the mosaic was dark and needed some light.

Years later the mosaic had become a conversation piece and when one was able to see the image of Jesus, it was pure magical.

At the age of 42 Ziggy's wife passed away. After her death he did experience other relationships, but he always made sure that the mosaic of Jesus Christ traveled with him where ever he went. At the age of 62 Ziggy met Annie.

What Ziggy found most appealing about Annie was her young spirit, her insight and creativity. In a very short time, they both developed strong feelings for one another and felt very connected. Their feelings for one another was so deep that within a few months they decided to move in together.

When Ziggy brought the Mosaic of Jesus over to their new home, Annie was very impressed with the mosaic and with how talented Ziggy was. When Annie slowly focused on the mosaic and saw Jesus in the picture she was in awe of its incredible beauty. However, Annie also noticed that the mosaic was very dark in colour and needed some light.

One day Annie asked Ziggy if she could somehow add some brightness to the picture. He immediately agreed with her, and told her to go ahead, add the light to Jesus. He also shared with her that he noticed the mosaic needed some kind of brightness the day he finished making it.

Before Annie started working on the mosaic she asked Ziggy why he made the mosaic so dark. He explained to her that the sufferings that Jesus went through were very dark moments for Him. Being a woman of faith, Annie completely understood what he meant.

Annie knew what Jesus truly stood for, and that was love, and love is the light which takes away the darkness. She then realized how important it was now to give Jesus light, the light of love. Annie then went ahead and gave the light to Jesus.

Before Annie started to give the mosaic a vision of luminance, she asked Ziggy if she could add some paint at the lower corner of the of the mosaic? Ziggy said to her that he was not comfortable with that idea. She did understand how Ziggy felt and agreed with him. We both understood that the mosaic of Jesus was a very special work of art.

Annie new at that point she had to come up with
another idea to give Jesus light. She then decided
to just put a light at the lower corner of the mosaic
which all of a sudden lit the mosaic up so perfectly.
After giving the mosaic light it made it look more
beautiful then ever; it actually gave it new life!

When looking at the mosaic Annie now felt very
connected to the image of Jesus. It also gave her an
extraordinary feeling of joy. Ziggy was then so
amazed at what Annie had done with the Mosaic,
and he also got the same feeling looking at the
peaceful loving light next to Jesus.

Ziggy and Annie then were so pleased at how the mosaic looked that they decided to take photos and even made greeting cards out of it. Inside of the greeting cards they wrote:

IF YOU CAN SEE ME, YOU WILL FEEL ME.

Now that Annie had given the light to the mosaic of Jesus, she became very inspired to write the book she had been planning to write for years. She used the beautiful picture of the mosaic for the front cover of her book.

When Annie mentioned to Ziggy that she wanted to use the picture of the mosaic for her book, he was pleasantly surprised, and told her that the book cover had taken the work of art to a new dimension. It now had even more meaning then when he first had made the mosaic of Jesus Christ.

After all these years, Ziggy's feelings of misery and hopelessness had now found a light of peace within him. That loving light had now regained his hope once again. He now realized that the light of love within him was much stronger than his feelings of darkness. Annie and Ziggy knew at that point that the Mosaic of Jesus Christ had a mission, a purpose and a destiny.

The Mosaic was made with feelings of love and darkness, and the Mosaic traveled with Ziggy for many years to finally meet his sweetheart Annie, so she could give Jesus light, and then the light of love would guide the mosaic to it's destiny, a book for all the world to see.

The Forgotten Light, I Am

Ziggy, at the time when he made the Mosaic.

Annie and Ziggy

Let Love Lead the way

Teachings of Jesus Christ

The teachings of Jesus Christ are life changing and timeless. When Jesus spoke, lives were transformed and the direction of life forever altered. He tells us that He is "the way, the truth and the life" (John 14:6), and His words have remarkable power. Whether you are just beginning to seek Jesus or have been a believer for years, the Word of God can always speak new truths into your life!
Most important teaching of Jesus is: "I am the way, the truth and the life. No one comes to the Father, except through me".

(John 14:6)

"For God so loved the world, that he gave his only Son, that whoever believes in him should not perish but have eternal life. For God did not send his Son into the world to condemn the world, but in order that the world might be saved through him. Whoever believes in him is not condemned, but whoever does not believe is condemned already, because he has not believed in the name of the only Son of God".

John 3:16

Sermon on the Mount

Jesus' teachings in his own words, from his Sermon on the Mount:

Blessed are the poor in spirit,
for theirs is the kingdom of heaven.
Blessed are those who mourn,
for they will be comforted.
Blessed are the meek,
for they will inherit the earth.
Blessed are those who hunger and thirst for
righteousness,
for they will be filled.
Blessed are the merciful,
for they will be shown mercy.
Blessed are the pure in heart,
for they will see God. Blessed are the peacemakers,
for they will be called sons of God.
Blessed are those who are persecuted because of
righteousness,
for theirs is the kingdom of heaven.
Blessed are you when people insult you, persecute
you and falsely say all kinds of evil against you
because of me.
Rejoice and be glad, because great is your reward in
heaven,
for in the same way they persecuted the prophets
who were before you.
Matt. 5:1-12

Let Us Not Forget God

We forget God's past works of salvation: "then take care lest you forget the Lord, who brought you out of the land of Egypt, out of the house of slavery"
Deuteronomy 6:12

We believe lies instead of the Word of God: "This is your lot, the portion I have measured out to you, declares the Lord, because you have forgotten me and trusted in lies"
Jeremiah 13:25

We are satisfied with the temporary need of the hour: "but when they had grazed, they became full, they were filled, and their heart was lifted up; there fore they forgot me"
Hosea 13:6

Believe that Christ has the power to change your life.

Prayer to accept Jesus into your life.

Dear Lord **Jesus**, I know that I am a sinner, and I ask for Your forgiveness. I believe You died for my sins and rose from the dead. I turn from my sins and invite You to come into my heart and life. I want to trust and follow You as my Lord and Savior.

"I am the way, the truth and the life. No one comes to the Father, except through me."

John 14:6

The Miracle Prayer

Lord Jesus, I come before you, just as I am, I am sorry for all my sins, I repent of my sins, please forgive me. In your name, I forgive all others for what they have done against me. I renounce Satan, evil spirits and all their works. I give you my entire self. Lord Jesus, now and forever, I invite you into my life Jesus, I accept you as my Lord, God and Saviour. Heal me, change me, strengthen me in body, soul and spirit.
Come Lord Jesus, cover me with your precious blood, and fill me with your Holy Spirit, I Love You Lord Jesus. I Praise You Jesus. I Thank You Jesus. I shall follow you every day of my life.
Amen.

▪▪

Say this Prayer faithfully, no matter how you feel, when you come to the point where you sincerely mean each word, with all your heart, something good spiritually will happen to you. You will experience Jesus, and HE will change your whole life in a very special way. You will see.

1993 Servite Fathers, O.S.M.

Sharing Your Faith
With Others

We all feel our own belief is the truth, and because we strongly feel this way, we want to share our faith with others. However, it is important to listen and learn about what other people believe in. By listening to others of the many different beliefs, we can become more enlightened in our own faith. If we first listen to others with love, respect and interest, we then will get the same love, respect and interest from them. It is not our responsibility to convince others to believe in our own truth.

Listen and share your beliefs with one another, and then leave it in God's hands to enlighten us with the Light of Truth.

All is on God's timing

The Forgotten Light

About The Author

Annie (birth name, Annita Quintieri) has a unique insight into personal behavior as a result of her years of experience as Beautician and a Fashion Designer and the confidence's that were shared in that capacity. This is further complemented by a degree in Social Services and her interaction with less privileged members of society which has given her an even greater depth of understanding of life's challenges and the growing need for greater spiritual awareness. Also, she has developed a deeper understanding of the inner self and the outer self and how one reflects on the other.

Throughout Annie's life she has pursued a better understanding about love and unity. In 2009, she got a message from a dream that inspired her to write books on Love and Unity.

Annie was born in Italy. She spent her early childhood in Italy and most of her adult life living in Toronto, Canada. She has only one son and a grandson, which now live in Italy.

Books by Annie Q. Porco

Keys to Unity
(Published by Balboa Press,
a division of Hay House)
Angel of Light
Unity for One God
Sweet Kisses
Sleeping Beauty of Love
Wishes After I'm Gone
SEVEN LOVES, Unconditional Love
Snow White and the Queen, Mirror, Mirror
The Magic of Kindness and Courage
Love and Light, Painting and Designs
Let Love Lead the Way
Daily Simple Reminders
Nine Steps to Donald J. Trump
ONE, Our God of Love
Journey to the Other Side
A Short Sweet Love Story

Made in the USA
Middletown, DE
18 January 2019